What Our Readers Have Said...

"The Pinpoint Training Series delivers information that could be used in a lot different areas."

•

"Applicable and valid. The information is good."

•

"I like this because I can take them with me to read at a convenient time. I feel the little time I have to spend in the office is best use on activities that directly relate to revenue opportunities. I like the short amount of time it takes to keep up with these."

•

"I like the fact that the format allows the books to be reviewed as time permits. All work has been conducted on personal, evening/weekend time."

•

"My thought is that the real value of these books comes into effect when doing the action plans."

•

"The challenge when I think a specific topic does not apply is to find a way to make it apply."

•

"Short and sweet. These books are easy to comprehend."

•

"These books are very easy to read and clearly outlined."

•

"I have enjoyed reading these books. They are relevant to today's work environment and the ongoing change in the way we manage our workforce."

•

"I believe the contents of the Pinpoint series are excellent. It causes one to reflect on the daily dynamics in working with oneself as well as with management and peers."

•

"Most of the information in these would help an open-minded management person, or an inexperienced management person."

•

"These books will pay for the time that I am investing. There are numerous good ideas that will streamline what I do and how I do it."

•

"All and all I think the Pinpoint series is a good program. I know other people I would love to have something like this. I think a lot of the suggestions are very useful, and can be applicable to everyday situations. If nothing else it's a good reference guide to fall back upon if a situation arises in the future."

•

"These books reinforce many concepts that I have learned through seminars, schooling and other programs. For myself, it serves as a constant learning tool that keeps me on top of the issues that many of us encounter every day."

•

"All in all, I think you have good training books. It helps everyone to review these materials, it serves as a good reminder to us on how to conduct ourselves."

•

"The information is valuable in these books."

•

Building & Nurturing Trust Among Salespeople

Pinpoint Sales Management Skill Development Training Series

TIMOTHY F. BEDNARZ

MAJORIUM
BUSINESS PRESS

Pinpoint Sales Management Skill Development Training Series
"Building & Nurturing Trust Among Salespeople"
Timothy F. Bednarz

Graphic design: Monika Pawlak

Majorium Business Press
2025 Main Street
Stevens Point, WI 54481
715.342.1018 • 800.654.4935

ISBN 978-1-62101-054-8

Printed in the United States of America

Introduction

The Pinpoint Sales Management Skill Development Training Series is designed for targeted training and education regarding increased improvement in a specific skill or competency.

Each book within this series is designed to be easy to use, understand and apply to your job. It can be used as a basis for training individuals, as a discussion guide or as a personal training tool.

Each chapter within this book discusses a specific concept. When you have completed all eight chapters you should have a 360° perspective of the topic.

Additionally, each chapter is divided into specific sections:

- The first section provides you with an overview of the topic
- The Implications section discusses why the concept is important, and why it is important to learn and apply.
- The Strategies, Tips & Techniques to Apply section teaches how to use and apply the particular concept to your work.
- The Points to Ponder section gives you something to think about or to be discussed with a group setting. These are questions not meant to be immediately answered, but to be pondered over time.
- The Training Activity section provides you with the tools to transfer what you have learned to your job. It is designed to help create an action plan to effectively apply the concept.

Each of the topics in this series is time-tested and proven in the marketplace. They have been used by thousands of employees as training tools. Many of the users have commented that what made these books valuable, was the ability to refer to them when a problem surfaced. They indicated that they remembered reading about the exact problem. They referred back to these books and found an appropriate solution.

You will find them equally valuable as a resource in your professional development library.

Table of Contents

LEARNING OBJECTIVES:

- Why trust is important.
- To effectively build and nurture trust.
- To identify the challenges of trust building.
- To analyze the consequences of mistrust and betrayal.

1

Defining the Role of Trust in Sales Management

As seen in numerous large-scale corporate scandals around the turn of the century, trust or a lack thereof has a dramatic impact on the organization. While an organization can be defined as trusting and empowering, it is the individuals within it who form the basis for these qualities.

The responsibility for fostering and nurturing trust does not lie with the bottom tiers of the organization, but the sales managers that lead it. Where there is no trust, there is no legitimacy to leadership.

The starting point is the personal commitment made by individual sales managers.

IMPLICATIONS — WHAT THIS MEANS TO YOU

Trust and empowerment stem from the individual actions of the sales manager. However, once initiated, trust and empowerment create a synergy within the organization that has the ability to move it forward to unimaginable heights.

As soon as salespeople know they can trust the words and actions of their sales managers, they are motivated. All too often the words sound good, but the accompanying actions do not follow, fostering a sense of mistrust and fear within salespeople.

Once sales managers have established trust with their salespeople, a strong bond is formed that is difficult to break. Unless trust is broken and people feel betrayed, salespeople will be intensely loyal and cooperate to achieve mutual goals and objectives. This is the strongest principle of leadership and its essence.

STRATEGIES, TIPS & TECHNIQUES TO APPLY

Whether or not a sales manager is trusted is determined by his or her actions. Anyone can make statements and pronouncements; it is by actions that an individual is judged. Sales managers must hold to higher standards of personal behavior if they are to foster and nurture trust with their salespeople, who closely observe every word and action.

Sales managers are judged by the following criteria:

Promises and Commitments

Corporate sales managers are placed under an enormous amount of stress and will miss commitments, especially minor ones made in the heat of daily activities. However, they pay close attention to what they say, and do what they promise. If unable to keep their commitment, they immediately inform the other party and make alternative arrangements.

Salespeople take note of a leader who makes a personal commitment but fails to keep it due to political or internal pressures. If when confronted with this failure they make excuses rather than take responsibility, they will be perceived as hypocritical. Salespeople with little other alternative may accept the excuse, but will inwardly feel betrayed and no longer trust the sales manager. The foundation for leadership has been greatly undermined.

Mistakes

As part of the human condition, everybody makes mistakes and fails. When leaders make mistakes, they often impact and affect their organization. Trust is established when sales managers openly acknowledge their mistakes to their salespeople and apologize for them.

Sales managers also allow their salespeople to experiment, make mistakes and fail without repercussions. They foster an atmosphere where salespeople can learn from their mistakes and move on. Sales managers understand that individuals can only grow when they are allowed to learn. The most effective learning experiences stem not from successes but failures and mistakes.

Loyalty

Sales managers give and demand loyalty from their salespeople. While they understand that loyalty is earned, they do not tolerate salespeople who are disloyal to their organization and each other.

The most open demonstration of a sales manager's own lack of loyalty can be seen in his or her constant and open criticism of superiors and salespeople in their absence. While loyalty is not blind, sales managers must demonstrate, at all times, a deep sense of allegiance to the organization, superiors, associates and salespeople.

If a sales manager takes issue with the actions of others, they should openly but privately discuss it with the individual and not criticize them behind his or her back.

Information

Sales managers as leaders show faith in their salespeople when they share information with them. In many organizations, the control of information is the basis of personal power. Sales managers understand that salespeople must be informed if they are to do their job well and be empowered to make decisions affecting their work. Those who withhold information clearly demonstrate mistrust of their salespeople.

Involvement

Trust is established with salespeople when they are included and empowered to make decisions that affect them. Trust is undermined when salespeople are enabled to make decisions but the decisions are never acted upon and implemented.

Effective sales managers actively work with their salespeople and have faith in their decisions. They work with their salespeople in implementing them and striving toward the accomplishment of mutual goals and objectives.

Recognition

Trust is fostered and nurtured when sales managers recognize the individual contributions of their salespeople and publicly recognize them for their efforts.

When new ideas and strategies work, sales managers who lead never accept the credit for the idea. They always acknowledge the efforts and contributions of their salespeople. To do otherwise betrays the trust of those salespeople.

Communications

Leaders build trust within their organization by maintaining open communication with all salespeople, superiors and associates. They understand that trust is only established when they communicate regardless of the situation and whether or not the information is positive or negative.

Goals and objectives are effectively met when all involved have a complete picture of what is happening around them, including the barriers and obstacles to be overcome.

Respect Confidentiality

Sales managers understand trust is developed when they respect and honor confidential and sensitive information provided to them by superiors, associates and salespeople.

They also know they must trust their salespeople with the confidential and sensitive information they need to do their jobs and make quality decisions. Without this confidence, sales managers will not be able to create a trusting environment since they are evincing a basic suspicion of their salespeople.

POINTS TO PONDER — SOMETHING TO THINK ABOUT

1. How would you rate your personal level of trustworthiness?
2. How would you evaluate the atmosphere in your organization?

TRAINING ACTIVITY — APPLICATION & ACTION PLAN

1. Perform a self-analysis regarding trust. On a sheet of paper list the following:
    - Promises and commitments
    - Mistakes
    - Loyalty
    - Information
    - Involvement
    - Credit
    - Communications
    - Respect confidentiality
2. Next to each category, list ways you can increase your personal levels of trust and foster trust with your salespeople.
3. Identify the actions you need to take to implement your ideas.

2

The Impact of Trust on an Sales Organization

The overall effects of trust reach deeply into any organization. Trust is the key element and core of leadership. It is the foundation upon which all other management competencies are based, and the basis for all human interaction at all levels, from salespeople to customers. Both motivation and loyalty are based upon trust. Sales managers and their organizations cannot function without it.

IMPLICATIONS — WHAT THIS MEANS TO YOU

Trust is at the heart of leadership. The faith placed in a leader by superiors, associates and salespeople stems directly from his or her personal trustworthiness. With the development of mutual trust, salespeople are motivated to take additional steps to support each other in the accomplishment of mutual goals and objectives.

The factors that establish and sustain trust can never be compromised. It is what defines a leader's character and competence. As a keystone of management, anything that diminishes mutual trust works to undermine and eventually destroy the ability to lead.

STRATEGIES, TIPS & TECHNIQUES TO APPLY

A sound organization is built upon a trusting environment. This builds strong relationships of faith in one another, empowerment, performance and a shared vision resulting in the following benefits:

Increased Personal Trust

Sales managers who develop a high-trust environment are working on multiple levels to create trust in themselves, superiors, associates, salespeople, suppliers and customers. They understand the establishment of trust begins with themselves, then flows to all levels of their organization. Trust is not an organizational function but a personal one. Once established, it can then be cultivated one individual at a time. It means keeping promises and honoring commitments, acknowledging mistakes, demonstrating loyalty, openly communicating with others and maintaining confidences.

Leadership demands that sales managers stand up for their personal values and beliefs despite potential negative consequences. When others see a sales manager's unwavering commitment, personal levels of trust and confidence increase. People know they are able to trust and believe a sales manager's words and actions. This is an immeasurable, priceless quality that can enable an organization to rise to great heights.

Strengthened Relationships

An environment of trust strengthens all personal relationships in the business. This occurs because as increasing levels of trust are reached, promises and commitments are kept, faith in and loyalty to each other are established, communication improved and mistakes openly acknowledged.

A synergy is established as individuals in the organization are bonded together by deeper levels of trust. Each develops an understanding that he or she can count on others to do their job and can deal with them openly, honestly and with integrity. This establishes an organizational cohesiveness that is indispensable to attaining mutual goals and objectives.

Improved Communication

Higher levels of trust beget better communication within the organization. In high-trust environments, information is shared with the people who need it at all levels because it is common knowledge they can be trusted to apply the information appropriately. Communication channels are also opened to include all levels of salespeople, regardless of their position or authority.

Improved communication in an environment of mutual trust allows both sales managers and salespeople to openly admit and acknowledge personal mistakes, learn from them and move on free of repercussion. It also acknowledges that salespeople at all levels can be trusted to honor confidential and sensitive information. This empowers salespeople and actively involves them in the decisions affecting them.

Sustained Positive Change

As trust and open communication are firmly rooted in the organizational culture, sales managers are able to effect ongoing positive change. This occurs as organizational cohesiveness is established and all salespeople are motivated by a shared vision of what the organization can realize through the attainment of mutual goals and objectives. All salespeople trust their leaders and organization to recognize their accomplishments and contributions and do not fear someone else being given credit for their work.

Decreased Frustrations

As a spirit of trust and open communication is achieved, sales managers will experience a decrease in frustrations and resistance as dysfunctional relationships are eliminated and group trust is established. Since salespeople at all levels are empowered and included in decision making, many problems are diminished and eliminated.

Increased Commitment

Increased levels of trust and organizational cohesiveness foster higher levels of commitment within the organization. As individual salespeople learn to work and trust each other as a unit, and see the positive results from their combined efforts, many will begin to contribute new ideas and feedback on how to better the organization. A synergy of trust, commitment and communication nurtures and sustains this positive momentum.

Reduction of Internal Politics

Internal politics, infighting and turf wars occur because individuals do not trust the organization to recognize and reward their contributions. Consequently, they begin to take control of their circumstances and use deceptive tactics to obtain what they feel is legitimately theirs.

An environment of trust eliminates or drastically reduces the negative impact of personal and internal politics. The atmosphere of trust bonds all sales managers and salespeople together and isolates parties who wish to be enmeshed in office politics. These individuals quickly learn that the rules have changed and that they must learn to cooperate rather than agitate—or leave the organization. The environment no longer tolerates time and energy-wasting internal politics since the focus has naturally shifted from the individual to the organization.

This does not imply individuals are consumed by and lost to the organization, only that as the provider of livelihoods its good is put first, and maneuvering, the rumor mill, backbiting and other game-playing are seen as useless pitfalls to avoid at all costs.

Improved Quality

The building of trust is the key to high-performing organizations. Strong and sustainable levels of trust transform the organization, increasing its effectiveness, productivity and the overall quality of the product or service being produced. This occurs because personal animosity and problems are eliminated or at least fade well into the background. Salespeople are motivated to increase the quality of their products and services because trust has empowered them to be a vital part of the organization. They are treated with respect and trusted to be a contributing part of the organization. This increases their personal satisfaction and loyalty to the organization.

POINTS TO PONDER — SOMETHING TO THINK ABOUT

1. What is the level of trust within the organizational unit that you lead?
2. Do you personally trust your superiors, associates and salespeople? Explain.

TRAINING ACTIVITY — APPLICATION & ACTION PLAN

1. Examine the key benefits of trust listed in this lesson and identify how increased trust can be beneficial to your organization within each area.
2. Determine how you can begin to increase individual levels of trust. Identify the actions you can personally take to establish an encompassing atmosphere of trust.

3

The Implications of Trust in the Workplace

The need for trust in the workplace and communication therein is understood by many leaders to be the foundational building block of the organization. The degree of trust developed will impact salesperson performance and retention, the development of teams and implementation of organizational change. Irrespective of size and industry, organizations are comprised of individuals who desire the same thing: the ability to trust those they work with. People cannot trust an organization, but they can trust their superiors, salespeople and associates.

IMPLICATIONS — WHAT THIS MEANS TO YOU

Issues of broken trust and personal betrayal are far from just the result of restructuring, downsizing, or other major organizational events. They are the product of the numerous micro-decisions that sales managers make every day. When individuals do not keep agreements or remain true to their word, do not share information or trust another salesperson's judgment or competence, trust is breached. Salespeople develop feelings of betrayal that lead to a chain of unresolved conflicts. These unresolved conflicts build a strong sense of mistrust and disloyalty that is extremely difficult to counteract.

This is important for sales managers because they are personally responsible for developing the trust needed to bind their organization together into a cohesive unit. They have the personal ability to control the series of micro-decisions that contribute to a sense of mistrust and undermine their ability to lead. With their personal words and actions, they have the power to build or destroy their salesperson's faith. They are the ones who must know that every statement or decision, no matter how inconsequential it may appear at the time, has an effect on whether or not corporate goals are reached.

STRATEGIES, TIPS & TECHNIQUES TO APPLY

Feelings of broken trust and betrayal are not just the byproducts of cataclysmic organizational change. They happen every day, and are in fact so pervasive that studies conducted since the mid-1940s have consistently shown that salespeople seem to crave the higher need for esteem, respect and self-actualization, while most employers feel concerned only for their salespeople's salary and safety. This demonstrates a clear disconnect that has implications for future organizations.

There is an increased need for trust in organizations as the world and corporate environments continue to change. Both organizational structures and sales managerial practices are continually changing, and these changes do not appear to be ending in the near-term. The policies and traditions that cemented salespeople to a company and which they relied upon have disappeared. They have all exacted a high price in the form of diminishing salesperson loyalty and trust.

Many sales managers will quickly attribute the lack of loyalty to salesperson job-hopping. Yet the 2001 *Randstad North American Salesperson Review* reported that 77% of salespeople polled defined success as "a long-term commitment with one company."

The lack of trust in many work environments is pervasive. While restructuring, mergers and acquisitions have produced opportunity, these changes also yield uncertainty and anxiety. Individuals in the current climate feel that they are unable to trust their future, their organization, or even themselves.

Sales managers need to create open and flexible organizations that are able to readily adapt to rapidly changing conditions. All indications point to organizational environments becoming more complex as changes and global pressures become more intense. While this places tremendous stress on the organization, sales managers must also respond to their salespeople's needs in a way that honors relationships and builds trust.

Change necessitates organizations to become agile and flexible. This requires salespeople who are willing to take risks. Taking risks requires salespeople that are able to trust themselves, their capabilities, and decisions as well as their leaders, coworkers and their organizations.

Sales managers must learn to evaluate their salespeople to determine their capacity for trust. This means establishing a foundation for trust that demands that past unsettled conflicts be resolved before a solid foundation for trust can be built. It also means that leaders must be conscious of their daily practices that either make or break salesperson trust.

The dynamics of trust are complex. It takes time and effort to develop trust, but one small event to lose it. Regaining lost trust, while extremely difficult, is a critical element in any relationship. By first trusting themselves and others, it is possible for sales managers to then develop caring, genuine relationships and rebuild trust with their salespeople.

When trust is ignored, the pain and price are tremendous as it is the key to all successful change initiatives within the organization. Without trust, change will be difficult if not impossible to achieve.

POINTS TO PONDER — SOMETHING TO THINK ABOUT

1. How critical do you perceive the element of trust to be within your organization?
2. Do you pay attention to the concept of trust or do you take it for granted?

TRAINING ACTIVITY — APPLICATION & ACTION PLAN

Consider the role of trust within your organization by examining your daily management practices.

1. Identify what are you doing to build trust with your salespeople.
2. Identify the actions that may be betraying your salesperson's trust.
3. Identify the actions and activities you can personally take to resolve past problems and build new levels of trust with your salespeople.

4

Common Pitfalls Associated with Trust Building in the Sales Environment

Sales managers can be so caught up in the flurry of daily tasks and activities that they easily stumble into many pitfalls resulting in broken trust with and betrayals of salespeople. Many of these actions are inadvertent, yet consequences can compound over time as unresolved conflicts build in salespeople's minds.

The desire for building trust is an attitude that sales managers either have or must develop if they wish to be successful. It is an essential building block of leadership. If sales managers are unable to nurture a workplace grounded in an appreciation for the power of trust, instead of lead they will only be able to control and direct using fear as the primary motivator.

IMPLICATIONS — WHAT THIS MEANS TO YOU

This is important for sales managers to appreciate because of the ease in which they can stumble into more outmoded management practices that undermine rather than cultivate salesperson trust. It may take time and effort to foster a personal attitude of trust, but when sales managers do they will find their people more effective, cooperative and productive. The alternative is an atmosphere of mistrust and betrayal where continual conflict, ineffectiveness and quality problems reign—and worsen over time.

STRATEGIES, TIPS & TECHNIQUES TO APPLY

Many sales managers can easily stumble into a myriad of pitfalls and practices that undermine their ability to build and foster trust with their salespeople. The stress and demands of daily work make it easy for sales managers to overlook many of their actions without understanding their attendant consequences. These can include:

Inconsistency

When sales managers are reactive rather than proactive, they are often inconsistent in their actions. A decision made in reaction to a specific event or circumstance can be inconsistent with a similar decision made at another time. While both may seem logical at the time, this inconsistency creates a sense of mistrust in salespeople since they have little or no idea what to expect from the leader's behavior.

Other inconsistencies occur when sales managers show favoritism toward one salesperson over another. Salespeople don't feel treated fairly and, consequently, will not trust the leader's judgment.

Reluctance to Share Information

Many sales managers are reluctant to share facts and figures with their salespeople because they feel unable to trust them with the information. This attitude clearly and completely sets the tone in the organization. If a sales manager shares information freely, he or she will find that salespeople will in turn begin to share information with them. This builds an atmosphere of mutual trust and open communication.

The sales manager reluctant to trust salespeople with information shuts down this critical two-way communication and limits the organization's ability to grow and adapt to change.

Lack of Personal Trust

Sales managers must learn to trust their own personal judgment and competency. They must accept that they will make mistakes, be willing to learn from them, and move on.

As sales managers face a daily barrage of information, feedback and data, they must learn to take time out of the day to do nothing but "let the dust settle." This enables them to see things more clearly and in their entirety, to identify what needs to be done, and as time spent with salespeople is usually more important than any other item on the agenda, where time needs to be spent in order to build trust.

Lack of Open Dialogue

Building or rebuilding trust among salespeople is one of the biggest challenges leaders face. Downsizing and mergers have taken their toll on workplace trust, making salespeople more territorial, wondering if they need to work to protect their jobs. Sales managers must acknowledge these fears and anxieties and open a dialogue allowing salespeople to vent.

Refusal to Deal with the Past

Many sales managers feel that the past events and circumstances that may have caused salespeople to feel betrayed are just that—in the past, and should be ignored. Yet it is a clear mistake to ignore these unresolved conflicts, as they will continue to fester and undermine any efforts to reestablish trust.

As sales managers open a dialogue with salespeople, these issues should be allowed to surface and be dealt with. While it is true that the past cannot be changed, these personal feelings must be resolved before trust can be truly established.

Lack of Clarity of Beliefs and Values

In the heat of organizational change, the beliefs and values of the organization can get lost or muddled. Sales managers must take the time to clarify fundamental beliefs and translate them into commonly held and agreed upon values. This allows them to align their organization with the company's values and beliefs.

POINTS TO PONDER — SOMETHING TO THINK ABOUT

1. What trust-building pitfalls give you the most trouble? Why?
2. What is the most successful way for you to build trust with your salespeople?

TRAINING ACTIVITY — APPLICATION & ACTION PLAN

In order to create more trusting relationships, and subsequently, more satisfaction:

1. Write down five things you have done in the last month to build trust in your workplace.
2. Write down five things you will do to build trust in the next thirty days.

5

Building a Foundation of Trust

The actions and behaviors of individual managers impact trust within the organization. Many fail to understand the elements of a trusting work atmosphere and the strategies used to build and establish a firm foundation for trust and management.

There are five key elements a sales manager must focus their efforts on to develop a comprehensive atmosphere of trust in their workplace. While the concept of trust implies participation by both the sales manager and the people they deal with, including their superiors, associates, peers and salespeople, it must start with the individual sales manager. It is counterproductive for sales managers to withhold their trust until they are able to trust the other party. In most cases trust is mutually developed by both parties and balanced by the commitment each brings to the relationship. Typically, salespeople and other individuals will reciprocate the trust placed in them by leaders.

IMPLICATIONS — WHAT THIS MEANS TO YOU

As sales managers attempt to build trust, they will experience reluctance in the form of salespeople who have felt betrayed by the organization in the past. Consequently, sales managers must signal a change by making the first steps to initiate and demonstrate trust in their salespeople. Once salespeople see that a true change has occurred, they will begin to slowly form the bonds of trust needed for leaders to be effective.

STRATEGIES, TIPS & TECHNIQUES TO APPLY

Sales managers who wish to establish a complete environment of trust with their superiors, associates, peers and salespeople must consider employing the following strategies:

Establish Professional and Personal Credibility

If leaders are credible, they are trusted by and believable to their salespeople. Salespeople consider a credible sales manager to be one who does not advance a personal agenda but has the best interests of the organization and his or her salespeople at heart.

Salespeople and other individuals view credibility from differing perspectives. Often credibility can be confused with personal competence. If the leader is knowledgeable and possesses both personal expertise and experience, they are considered credible. Conversely, sales managers who maintain positions in which they demonstrate professional incompetence, exhibit a lack of professional credibility, with salespeople viewing their direction, judgment and leadership as suspect.

The other aspect is the sales manager's own personal credibility. This involves the salesperson's ability to personally trust what they say or do. An individual may possess professional credibility and not possess the personal credibility to lead the organization. Strategies sales managers must apply to develop and foster personal credibility include:

- Making themselves available to their salespeople and easy to talk with. Good leaders do not wait for their salespeople to approach them, but seek them out on a regular basis. Many will walk around and talk with each salesperson several times a day to discuss everyday concerns and issues. This proactive approach allows them to monitor the pulse of their organization while facilitating open communication with their salespeople. They instantly address questions with straight answers and openly make their expectations of the organization and their salespeople known.
- Trusting their salespeople to handle their jobs and responsibilities

without regularly looking over their shoulders and micro-managing their activities.

- They are completely reliable and always deliver on their promises and commitments without fail, enabling salespeople to know without question that they can count on the leader.

Fairness

Trust is built when salespeople know their sales manager is fair and consistent in his or her actions, decisions and judgments—no matter who is involved and what the circumstances.

Fairness is comprised of both equity and consistency. Sales managers can use the following strategies to develop a strong sense of equity including:

- Ensure all salespeople are treated in the same manner.
- Make sure all actions, judgments and decisions are fair to all parties concerned.
- Avoid any favoritism among salespeople, especially where rewards, recognition and promotions are concerned.

Effective leaders make certain their actions, judgments and decisions are consistent and not based upon specific circumstances. Only when sales managers demonstrate consistency over time can they build trust with salespeople, who then know they will always be treated fairly.

Respect

Trust is built upon a foundation of mutual respect for one another. If respect is absent, trust can never be achieved. Sales managers can develop and foster respect with the following:

- Demonstrate a personal regard for individual salespeople's experience, expertise, knowledge, insight and perspectives concerning their jobs.
- Actively seek feedback and salespeople's insight, perspective and opinions regarding important decisions.
- Actively involve salespeople in the decision making process.

- Demonstrate appreciation for salespeople's personal contributions to the success of the organization.
- Provide the training, resources and support salespeople need to competently perform their jobs.
- Demonstrate care and concern for salespeople's lives outside of the workplace.

Pride

Trust is fostered and nurtured by a sense of mutual pride in the work, quality and accomplishments of the organization. This builds organizational cohesiveness that bonds all salespeople together and strengthens trust in all involved. As workplace cohesiveness increases, so does a sense of trust in the organization and its people. Everyone feels they are working together and each can be trusted to fulfill his or her role and responsibilities.

Sales managers can encourage the development of pride by using the following strategies:

- Help salespeople understand their individual role in the organization and how their efforts contribute to its success.
- Help them understand that they personally make a difference within the organization.
- Exhort salespeople to take satisfaction both in their organization's accomplishments and its contributions to their community.

Comradery

Comradery is not normally associated with the concept of trust, yet it does contribute to the organizational cohesiveness established by trust. As cited above, the stronger the organizational cohesiveness, the stronger the bond between leaders and salespeople. All involved feel linked by common goals, experiences and successes. They have a sense that everyone is "in it together," and work as a unit rather than as individuals.

Sales managers can use the following strategies to build comradery with their salespeople:

- Create a workplace where a common concern is demonstrated and salespeople feel they can "be themselves."
- Openly and regularly celebrate special events and mutual successes.
- Consistently and openly recognize, reward and celebrate individual successes in a warm and genuine manner.

POINTS TO PONDER — SOMETHING TO THINK ABOUT

1. Have you considered the five components discussed to be part of an atmosphere of trust?
2. Can you see how if one of the components is missing, trust is undermined?

TRAINING ACTIVITY — APPLICATION & ACTION PLAN

1. Evaluate the atmosphere of trust within your organization.
2. Take a sheet of paper and list the following components:
    - Credibility
    - Fairness
    - Respect
    - Pride
    - Comradery
3. Objectively evaluate the prevalence of each component in turn.
4. Identify gaps and determine the specific strategies needed to address them.

6

When Trust Is Missing

There are many companies and organizations where the concept of trust is either considered unimportant and overlooked out of ignorance or has been damaged or destroyed by acts of betrayal by both managers and employees. The ramifications of a missing or destroyed sense of trust can be far-reaching in terms of wasted human capital and negative impact on the company's bottom line.

An atmosphere where trust is damaged or absent is characterized by a lack of confidence, respect, pride and organizational cohesiveness. The consequences of these missing components are conflict, unrest, instability and an overall lack of effectiveness, efficiency and productivity.

Undoubtedly there are sales managers who thrive in this atmosphere. Most employ a "divide and conquer" management philosophy in order to gain an illusion of personal control and power. This approach thrives on salespeople's misery and unhappiness to satisfy personal agendas, and is wholly incompatible with an empowered organization.

IMPLICATIONS — WHAT THIS MEANS TO YOU

This is important for sales managers as leaders, because without creating trust, they cannot guide and direct their organization to greater heights of effectiveness and productivity. Empowered sales managers are the antithesis of the divide and conquer sales manager who is only interested in the power and control they can garner irrespective of the price paid by their people and their company.

STRATEGIES, TIPS & TECHNIQUES TO APPLY

When sales managers fail to create and foster an atmosphere of trust or allow it to be damaged or destroyed, they are surrendering their leadership role, as its basis has been effectively removed. Instead they have taken the mantle of a director and controller in an organization plagued by:

Increased Conflict

Lack of credibility, respect and fairness is a breeding ground for every conceivable form of conflict. In the absence of trust, an "us vs. them" atmosphere prevails where salespeople don't believe the words and actions of management. This results in varying levels of labor unrest.

Additionally, lack of trust creates personal conflicts and problems both between leaders and subordinates and among salespeople. It forces sales managers to waste time settling petty disputes and babysitting salesperson problems. This saps their ability to focus on the more important issues impacting productivity and profitability.

Lack of Communication

Diminished or nonexistent trust affects overall communication in the organization. Since management doesn't trust salespeople, they are reluctant to share important information with them. Additionally, salespeople are resistant to sharing their own information, insights and perspectives that can help management make more qualified decisions ultimately leading to a better product or service. As problems persist, communication continues to suffer.

Increased Gossip

The vacuum created by a lack of communication is filled by harmful, toxic rumors. Individual reputations are damaged and overall performance is diminished by the effects of gossip among salespeople. Since salespeople feel they cannot trust either the company or its sales managers, their trust is placed in rumor and innuendo. This can completely undermine the effectiveness and cohesion of an organization.

Increased Personal Problems

When the working environment is destabilized by an atmosphere void of trust, companies experience an increase in absenteeism, salesperson turnover, theft, sabotage, lawsuits and a host of other problems that bleed the company's time, effectiveness, profitability and resources. As these problems continue and fester, mistrust is compounded—and plunges the company into deeper and more looming difficulties.

This atmosphere often leads more quality salespeople to leave for a more stable working environment, leaving behind problematic salespeople who only cause further difficulties for the company.

Increased Quality Problems

As problems continue, salesperson attitudes and morale are affected, resulting in a decrease in overall product quality. This ultimately impacts the customer and can result in a marked loss of business.

Since the atmosphere of mistrust fosters poor morale and personal attitudes, salespeople lose their sense of pride, organizational cohesiveness and comradery. Concern over the loss of business and profitability is replaced by self-serving preservation of personal power and job security.

The overall result can be a death spiral for a company unless leadership can rebuild trust and restore its former status as a quality provider of products or services.

Reduced Productivity

The ultimate result of a lack of trust is an overall loss of productivity. In some instances, problems have become so overwhelming for a company that facilities have been closed, jobs lost and operations shifted to other locations or outside of the country.

The impact of a loss of trust and its ramifications cannot be overemphasized because of the dramatic and often overwhelming effect it can have on the organization. It not only can undermine the ability to lead, but ultimately can lead to an organization's downfall.

POINTS TO PONDER — SOMETHING TO THINK ABOUT

1. What have been your experiences when trust was missing or destroyed by betrayal?
2. Have you ever betrayed your salespeople's trust? What were the consequences?

TRAINING ACTIVITY — APPLICATION & ACTION PLAN

1. Evaluate your own organization to determine if you can identify problems or potential problems in each of the following areas:
    - Increased conflict
    - Lack of communication
    - Increased gossip
    - Increased personal problems
    - Increased quality problems
    - Reduced productivity
2. Identify specific actions that must be taken to eliminate these problems before they turn into major crises within your company.

7

How the Principles of Trust Building Influences Decision Making

Trust-building has more far-reaching implications than any other factor in the workplace. This is especially true where decision making is concerned. Sales managers are making decisions that impact salespeople and customers alike and that define the organization in their eyes. Leadership depends upon a sales manager's ability to generate trust and credibility in his or her words and actions.

IMPLICATIONS — WHAT THIS MEANS TO YOU

Trust and credibility are the basis of leadership. These elements are defined by the decisions a sales manager makes. Leaders are fully aware of the impact their decisions have upon their ability to effectively lead their organization. Inconsistent, faulty or poor decision making skills will undermine any trust and credibility they have developed.

If salespeople cannot trust the words and actions of their sales manager, he or she does not have the ability to lead. There is no basis for effective management. As individuals in this position motivate only with fear and intimidation, they will produce minimal results.

STRATEGIES, TIPS & TECHNIQUES TO APPLY

Decision making is a complex process, even when decisions appear simple. Sales managers automatically go through a process that takes into consideration a series of factors involved in the development of a fair and balanced decision.

Truth

Before they make any determination, leaders must make sure they are dealing with the facts surrounding a situation or an event—not subjective opinions and perceptions. This includes ensuring all parties affected by a specific decision agree not only upon the pertinent facts but also the veracity of the way in which the situation has been portrayed.

Arriving at an agreement on the truth of an issue is not as simple as it may seem. Personal agendas and internal politics can often alter one's view of the truth and taint the entire process. Leaders must become adept at objective fact-finding and develop the personal skills to separate reality from opinion.

Without this critical element, most decisions, based upon supposition rather than fact, will be faulty.

Credible

Leaders must not only examine the truth of the available facts but also the credibility of the information and its sources. It is not uncommon for information presented as truth to be based upon rumor and supposition. While the information is perceived as truthful, it is not considered credible due to unreliable sources. Consequently sales managers must not only consider the reliability of the information presented to them but also the credibility of the source.

Fair

Sales managers who lead must ensure that any decisions they make are equitable to all involved. This means that no favoritism is shown toward one party over another and that the consequence of a decision, whether positive or negative, impacts all individuals equally.

When decisions are made that do in fact impact one party more than another, leaders must assure that the criteria used for making their decision treats all parties fairly without bias or partiality.

Respect

Sales managers must assure that when making decisions, all interested people are given equal opportunity and access to make their case. Sales managers should respect their feedback, insights, opinions and perspectives, and give them equal consideration during the decision making process.

Comradery

An additional ramification of a leader's decision making is the impact on comradery within the organization. When sales managers make decisions fairly and without bias, they should enhance comradery in the organization. This occurs because the credibility of the decision is enhanced and it is considered fair, truthful, and to promote good will throughout the organization.

Beneficial

The final aspect of the principles of trust in decision making is the need for sales managers as leaders to make certain that their decisions are beneficial to all individuals concerned, without bias or favoritism.

Rotary International promotes an easy to remember decision making tool. The use of this tool builds trust and ethical decision making and incorporates all of the elements discussed in this lesson.

The FOUR-WAY TEST of the things we think, say or do:

1. Is it the TRUTH?
2. Is it FAIR to all concerned?
3. Will it build GOODWILL and BETTER FRIENDSHIPS?
4. Will it be BENEFICIAL to all concerned?

POINTS TO PONDER — SOMETHING TO THINK ABOUT

1. Do you as a habit consider all of the elements of truth in your decision making?
2. What additional elements do you include in your decision making?

TRAINING ACTIVITY — APPLICATION & ACTION PLAN

Apply the Four-Way Test to all of your decisions for the next thirty days and determine if it has an impact.

1. Is it the TRUTH?
2. Is it FAIR to all concerned?
3. Will it build GOODWILL and BETTER FRIENDSHIPS?
4. Will it be BENEFICIAL to all concerned?

8

Trust Impacts Organizational Cohesiveness

The concept of organizational cohesiveness is recognized in the military as a factor that makes or breaks unit effectiveness. Military leaders have long recognized that when cohesiveness breaks down and is left unaddressed, the unit's ability to perform is not only diminished but ultimately destroyed. The same concept applies within organizations.

Organizational cohesiveness is achieved when all members of the organization have reached the point where they are working closely together as a single unit toward the accomplishment of mutual goals and objectives without regard for personal agendas and attitudes.

IMPLICATIONS — WHAT THIS MEANS TO YOU

By establishing trust leaders take a diverse collection of individuals and blend them into an efficient working unit. When this occurs, and leaders have built and are nurturing organizational cohesiveness, they will have accomplished their primary goals. This is a most satisfying and beneficial position for leaders to be in.

Leaders build and foster trust not only between their employees and themselves, but also between all members of the organizational unit. Cohesiveness is established and is reinforced over time because bonds of trust between individual members of the organization are strengthened. Each individual learns how he or she is able to trust the other members in the attainment of individual and organizational goals.

When sales managers as leaders are able to establish strong organizational cohesiveness, the following elements are found:

Teamwork

When organizational cohesiveness is achieved, sales managers see an overall increase in team development. Individual salespeople are able to work in self-directed groups to tackle specific problems, concerns and issues that need to be resolved if the organization is to progress and meet its objectives.

In many organizations, this is a major shift in thinking and personal attitudes. Salespeople and leaders think in terms of the team and organization, replacing their own personal goals and agendas with those of the organization.

Individual Contribution

It has been recognized that any individual within any company or organization can contribute ideas and insights as to how to improve quality, performance and productivity in the position they hold. Yet these individuals are generally reluctant to volunteer this information, primarily because they have not been asked in the past, and have therefore concluded their contributions are unwanted.

When organizational cohesiveness is achieved, many of these barriers are removed, and sales managers will see an overall increase in individual salesperson contributions. Since they are motivated by the success of the team or organization, they feel more open to contribute feedback, observations, insights, perspectives and ideas to assist them. When this occurs, and more individuals are motivated to personally contribute, a synergy is achieved that amplifies the power of these ideas, increases brainstorming, and infuses the organization with new and creative thinking.

Empowerment

A workplace environment that is built on trust and thus fosters organizational cohesiveness, also builds empowered salespeople. The sense of trust between sales managers and salespeople empowers them to make more independent decisions and work more freely in groups and teams since they are working toward common organizational goals and objectives. The concepts of trust and empowerment are codependent, feeding and building upon each other, strengthening over time.

Cooperation

While teamwork, empowerment and organizational cohesion all require collaboration between sales managers and salespeople as well as among salespeople themselves, within a cohesive organizational unit, there are levels of cooperation between individuals, departments, vendors and customers that cannot be minimized. These levels of cooperation are beyond the scope of individual responsibilities, yet are clearly visible and significantly contribute to the success of the organization. They are reflective of "team spirit," organizational pride and salesperson comradery. It is noticed by outsiders, helps define the organization and is the first thing to suffer when organizational cohesiveness is disrupted or destroyed.

Sales managers should note this sense of cooperation when they have achieved effective levels of organizational cohesiveness and then actively monitor it as an overall indicator of unit, division or company health.

Quality

Another easily discernable benefit of organizational cohesiveness is the increase in the quality of unit work and individual contributions. The organization has been able to maximize its efficiency, as an increase in overall product or service quality often translates into fewer defective and rejected units. This reduces the time required to rework faulty units, and increases the organization's efficiency and profitability.

POINTS TO PONDER — SOMETHING TO THINK ABOUT

1. Are you committed to the development of a cohesive organizational unit?
2. Can you see the benefits of working within a cohesive organizational unit?

TRAINING ACTIVITY — APPLICATION & ACTION PLAN

Examine your organizational unit and identify the specific barriers preventing you from building and nurturing organizational cohesion.

1. Consider the areas of trust, credibility, teamwork, empowerment, individual contributions and cooperation, and isolate difficulties that are preventing you or the organization from achieving cohesiveness.
2. Determine how you can remove or minimize the obstacles you have discovered.
3. Create an action plan to move your organization forward and increase overall cohesiveness.

About the Author

Timothy F. Bednarz, Ph.D. is CEO of the American Management Development Group, Inc. For over 20 years he has researched, designed and authored hundreds of learning and development programs used by Fortune 1000 companies.

He is also the author of *Great! What Makes Leaders Great. What They Did, How They Did It and What You Can Learn from It* (2011).

Speaking Availability

Timothy F. Bednarz, Ph.D. is available for speaking engagements for your next meeting or association event. He can be contacted at 800-654-4935 or by e-mail at timothy.bednarz@majorium.com.

Bulk Sales

Bulk sales of this book or any other titles available from Majorium Business Press. Inquiries can be directed to sales@majorium.com, or by phone at 800-6654-4935.

Quick Order Form

Fax orders: 715-342-1118. Send this form.

Telephone orders: Call 800-654-4935 toll-free. Have your credit card ready.

Email orders: sales@majorium.com

Postal orders: Majorium Business Press, 2025 Main Street, Stevens Point, WI 54481, USA.

Please send the following books:

____

____

____

____

Please send more FREE information on:

❑Catalog ❑Speaking/Seminars ❑Mailing Lists ❑Consulting

Name: ____

Address: ______________________________________

City: ____________________ State: _____ Zip: ________

Telephone: ____________________________________

Email address: ________________________________

Sales tax: Please add 5.5% for products shipped to Wisconsin addresses.

Shipping by air:

United States: $4.00 for first book and $2.00 for each additional product.

International: $9.00 for first book; $5.00 for each additional product (estimate).

Made in United States
Orlando, FL
04 November 2026

90202069R00028